You Can Become A

master soul winner

How to lead people to Jesus!

Daniel King

You Can Become a Master Soul Winner
How to lead people to Jesus!
By Daniel King

© 2008 Daniel King. All Rights Reserved.

King Ministries International
PO Box 701113
Tulsa, OK 74170 USA

1-877-431-4276

www.kingministries.com

daniel@kingministries.com

Table of Contents

Introduction • 7

One • 11
Soul Winners recognize Jesus
was a MASTER SOUL WINNER.

Two • 12
Soul Winners realize that the followers
of Jesus become MASTER SOUL WINNERS
by following His example.

Three • 13
Soul Winners NEED to go where the lost are.

Four • 17
Soul Winners witness even when it is INCONVENIENT.

Five • 18
Soul Winners recognize OPPORTUNITIES to witness.

Six • 20
Soul Winners TARGET THE LOST
with their prayer and witnessing.

Seven • 22
Soul Winners ENGAGE people in conversations.

Eight • 24
Soul Winners refuse to make EXCUSES for not witnessing.

Bonus Section • 25
Excuses that STOP people from Soul Winning

Nine • 27
Soul Winners talk with those who are DIFFERENT.

Ten • 29
Soul Winners leave their COMFORT ZONE
and reach into other people's worlds.

Table of Contents Cont...

Eleven • 31
Soul Winners turn the CONVERSATION towards God.

Twelve • 33
Soul Winners tap into their SPIRITUAL GIFTING.

Thirteen • 36
Soul Winners ignore attempts
to start a spiritual ARGUMENT.

Bonus Section • 38
Common Objections and Biblical Answers

Fourteen • 43
Soul Winners REVEAL JESUS to the hurting.

Fifteen • 45
Soul Winners know that the NEWLY
SAVED are the best evangelists.

Sixteen • 46
Soul Winners know that every person can make a DIFFERENCE.

Seventeen • 47
Soul Winners realize that soul winning is the
most IMPORTANT activity on earth.

Eighteen • 50
Soul Winners know that all of HEAVEN IS WATCHING.

Nineteen • 52
Soul Winners are PASSIONATE about
leading the lost to Christ.

Twenty • 54
The Soul Winner knows he or she is like a FARMER.

Bonus Section • 55
Four "L"-ements of the Harvest

Table of Contents Cont...

Twenty-One • 57
Soul Winners are NEVER DISCOURAGED
when a person is not saved immediately.

Twenty-Two • 58
Soul Winners know that their witnessing
will produce GREAT FRUIT.

Twenty-Three • 60
Soul Winners build a BIG
MONUMENT with their labors.

Twenty-Four • 62
Soul Winners aim to "SAVE THE MAN!"

Twenty-Five • 63
Soul Winners FOLLOW UP on the fruit.

Twenty-Six • 68
Soul Winners know EVERYONE MUST
MEET JESUS for themselves.

Twenty-Seven • 69
Soul Winners know the power of PRINTED MATERIAL.

Twenty-Eight • 71
Soul Winners know that JESUS IS
THE SAVIOR of the World.

Twenty-Nine • 72
Soul Winners know they will be HEROES IN HEAVEN.

Bonus Section • 74
Witnessing Tips/ Sample Script for Witnessing

Gospel Festival Pictures • 76-79

Special Product Offers • 80-81

About the Author • 83

Introduction

Jesus was a Master Soul Winner. The greatest soul-winning story in the Bible is when Jesus encounters a Samaritan woman in the fourth chapter of John. From His example, we can learn to become master soul winners ourselves.

Proverbs 11:30 says, "Those who win souls are wise." I believe soul winning is one of the greatest activities we can participate in as a believer. However, statistics show that 95% of Christians have never personally led another person to Jesus Christ. Soul winning is one of the most talked about ministries in the church, and unfortunately the most neglected. Soul winning is the one ministry that is available to all believers, but it is also one of the most difficult ministries to get people involved in. If you want to tell people about Jesus, but you are not sure what to say or how to say it, this book teaches you the how-to's of personal evangelism.

This book will endeavor to answer some of the common questions people ask about soul winning:
* Am I called to be a soul winner?
* How can I be an effective soul winner?
* How can I find opportunities to be a soul winner?
* What should I say when I witness?
* How can I lead my family members to Christ?
* How should I handle people who just want to argue about religion?

If you will put the principles of this book into practice in your life, you can become a master soul winner, just like Jesus.

John 4

¹Therefore, when the Lord knew that the Pharisees had heard that Jesus made and baptized more disciples than John ²(though Jesus Himself did not baptize, but His disciples), ³He left Judea and departed again to Galilee. ⁴But He needed to go through Samaria. ⁵So He came to a city of Samaria which is called Sychar, near the plot of ground that Jacob gave to his son Joseph. ⁶Now Jacob's well was there. Jesus therefore, being wearied from His journey, sat thus by the well. It was about the sixth hour. ⁷A woman of Samaria came to draw water. Jesus said to her, "Give Me a drink." ⁸For His disciples had gone away into the city to buy food. ⁹Then the woman of Samaria said to Him, "How is it that You, being a Jew, ask a drink from me, a Samaritan woman?" For Jews have no dealings with Samaritans. ¹⁰Jesus answered and said to her, "If you knew the gift of God, and Who it is who says to you, "Give Me a drink," you would have asked Him, and He would have given you living water." ¹¹The woman said to Him, "Sir, You have nothing to draw with, and the well is deep. Where then do You get that living water? ¹²Are You greater than our father Jacob, who gave us the well, and drank from it himself, as well as his sons and his livestock?" ¹³Jesus answered and said to her, "Whoever drinks of this water will thirst again,¹⁴but whoever drinks of the water that I shall give him will never thirst. But the water that I shall give him will become in him a fountain of water springing up into everlasting life." ¹⁵The woman said to Him, "Sir, give me this water, that I may not thirst, nor come here to draw." ¹⁶Jesus said to her, "Go, call your husband, and come here." ¹⁷The woman answered and said, "I have no husband." Jesus said to her, "You have well said, "˜I have no husband," ¹⁸for you have had five husbands, and the one whom you now have is not your husband; in that you spoke truly." ¹⁹The woman said to Him, "Sir, I perceive that You are a prophet. ²⁰Our fathers worshiped on this mountain, and you Jews say that in Jerusalem is the place where one ought to worship." ²¹Jesus said to her, "Woman, believe Me, the hour is coming when

you will neither on this mountain, nor in Jerusalem, worship the Father. ²²You worship what you do not know; we know what we worship, for salvation is of the Jews. ²³But the hour is coming, and now is, when the true worshipers will worship the Father in spirit and truth; for the Father is seeking such to worship Him. ²⁴God is Spirit, and those who worship Him must worship in spirit and truth." ²⁵The woman said to Him, "I know that Messiah is coming" (who is called Christ). "When He comes, He will tell us all things." ²⁶Jesus said to her, "I who speak to you am He." ²⁷And at this point His disciples came, and they marveled that He talked with a woman; yet no one said, "What do You seek?" or, "Why are You talking with her?" ²⁸The woman then left her waterpot, went her way into the city, and said to the men, ²⁹"Come, see a Man who told me all things that I ever did. Could this be the Christ?" ³⁰Then they went out of the city and came to Him. ³¹In the meantime His disciples urged Him, saying, "Rabbi, eat." ³²But He said to them, "I have food to eat of which you do not know." ³³Therefore the disciples said to one another, "Has anyone brought Him anything to eat?" ³⁴Jesus said to them, "My food is to do the will of Him who sent Me, and to finish His work. ³⁵Do you not say, 'There are still four months and then comes the harvest'? Behold, I say to you, lift up your eyes and look at the fields, for they are already white for harvest! ³⁶And he who reaps receives wages, and gathers fruit for eternal life, that both he who sows and he who reaps may rejoice together. ³⁷For in this the saying is true: 'One sows and another reaps.' ³⁸I sent you to reap that for which you have not labored; others have labored, and you have entered into their labors." ³⁹And many of the Samaritans of that city believed in Him because of the word of the woman who testified, "He told me all that I ever did." ⁴⁰So when the Samaritans had come to Him, they urged Him to stay with them; and He stayed there two days. ⁴¹And many more believed because of His own word. ⁴²Then they said to the woman, "Now we believe, not because of what you said, for we ourselves have heard Him and we know that this is indeed the Christ, the Savior of the world." ⁴³Now after the two days He departed from there and went to Galilee. *(NKJV)*

Soul Winners recognize Jesus was a MASTER SOUL WINNER.

"Therefore, when the Lord knew that the Pharisees had heard that Jesus made and baptized more disciples than John…" (John 4:1)

John the Baptist had baptized thousands. Jesus baptized even more. Everywhere Jesus went He led people to God the Father. He was such a great soul winner that the religious leaders of His day were upset because He was much more effective than they were.

Soul winning was Christ's primary purpose. The reason Jesus came to earth was to save the lost. "…Christ Jesus came into the world to save sinners…" (1 Timothy 1:15) "The Son of Man has come to seek and to save that which was lost." (Luke 19:10) Jesus was a soul winner, the greatest soul winner the world has ever seen.

In this book you will discover why Jesus reached out to the Samaritan woman at the well. By ministering to her, He was fulfilling His purpose. He did not come to entertain, or to make money, or to build a big ministry. No, He was passionate about rescuing mankind from the pit of hell. His passion should be our driving passion too.

Soul Winners realize that the followers of Jesus become MASTER SOUL WINNERS by following His example.

"...though Jesus Himself did not baptize, but His disciples." (John 4:2)

So many people responded to the teaching of Jesus that the disciples were needed to help baptize the new converts. From the very beginning of His ministry, Jesus taught His disciples how to be soul winners. We also learn to be soul winners by following His example.

Jesus is our example, and He demonstrated in His life the proper methods for effective soul winning. His methods and techniques are our example. Jesus desired for all His followers to become master soul winners too. The first words He spoke to His disciples were, "Follow Me, and I will make you fishers of men." (Matthew 4:19) The final instructions He gave were, "Go therefore and make disciples of all the nations..." (Matthew 28:19) If you are a true disciple of Jesus, then you will be a soul winner.

You are called to be a soul winner. Jesus commanded all His disciples, "Go into all the world and preach the Gospel to every creature." (Mark 16:15 KJV) All you need to do to become a master soul winner is to follow the example of Jesus.

3

Soul Winners NEED to go where the lost are.

"Jesus left Judea and departed again to Galilee. But He needed to go through Samaria." (John 4:3-4)

Usually, any Jews traveling from Judea to Galilee would have avoided Samaria. Even though the most direct route goes through Samaria, most Jews deliberately walked around this entire area. But Jesus "needed" to go through Samaria. Why did Jesus need to go to Samaria? Because He knew there was a woman who needed help. If we are going to be soul winners, we have to be willing to step outside our normal patterns of living. We must go to where the lost are.

Non-Christians do not typically go to church. We are commanded to preach the good news to every person. If the unsaved do not come to us, we must go to them. We must go outside the four walls of the church and approach people where they are. We should evangelize the unreached, the unchristian, the unloved. Far too many Christians stay in the church, the classroom, and the pew instead of going out into the street, the neighborhoods, and the malls where the people are. One evangelist said, "The strength of a church is not in how many it seats but in how many it sends." The measure of a church is not in how many go to the church, but how many go out from the church. We must think outside the walls.

Let's look at what the early disciples did. "Daily in the temple, and in every house, they did not cease teaching and preaching Jesus as the Christ." (Acts 5:42 NKJV) Notice they were preaching in the temple and in every house. The believers were going from house to house talking to every person who would listen.

Every believer is called to be involved in soul winning. It is not just a job for the pastor of the church. It would be a strange army that only sent out generals to fight. In the early church, "…The Lord added to the church daily those who were being saved." (Acts 2:47 KJV) I believe people should be added to your church daily as well. I am sure your pastor gives a great altar call on Sunday mornings and during your mid-week service. But, Sunday and Wednesday are only two days of the week. How will people get saved the other five days of the week unless every church member is actively sharing his or her faith?

The Story of the Elephant and the Ants

In Africa an industrious ant colony was regularly attacked by a rogue elephant. Every time the ants finished building their giant anthill, the elephant would destroy it with his massive feet.

One day the ants were so tired of rebuilding that they called an action committee meeting. They decided to defend their home by climbing a tree together. When the elephant passed by underneath, they planned to jump from the tree, land on the elephant, and sting it to death.

So, they put their plan into motion. They climbed the tree and as the elephant was walking by, the leader gave the signal. All the ants jumped down onto the elephant's back below. But the elephant just shook his huge body and all the ants went flying off.

The ants were all discouraged but then they looked up and saw one ant was still miraculously clinging to the elephant's massive neck. The ants started jumping up and down and shouting, "Choke him! Choke him!"

Sometimes pastors and ministers feel just like that ant that was attempting to choke the elephant to death. We are trying to save the world, meanwhile all the people in the church are shouting, "Get people saved! Get people saved!" but doing nothing to help out themselves.

It takes more than one person to save the world! The pastor and evangelist cannot reach the whole world by themselves; we need your help.

Eric Liddell, the great Olympic runner and missionary to China, said, "We are all missionaries. Wherever we go, we either bring people nearer to Christ, or we repel them from Christ." You do not need to study for years at a seminary to be an effective minister. All you need to do is share with people what God has done for you. Jesus chose ordinary men and women to be His followers. His disciples were not professional ministers with doctoral degrees. No, they were normal people like you and me. You are a witness. You have a testimony. If God has ever done a miracle in your life, you are qualified to be a minister. Ministry is simply telling people, "This is what God did for me, and what He did for me, I know He will do for you!"

> **Ministry is simply telling people, "This is what God did for me, and what He did for me, I know he will do for you!"**

4

Soul Winners witness even when it is INCONVENIENT.

"So He came to a city of Samaria which is called Sychar, near the plot of ground that Jacob gave to his son Joseph. Now Jacob's well was there. Jesus therefore, being wearied from His journey, sat thus by the well. It was about the sixth hour. A woman of Samaria came to draw water." (John 4:5-7)

In ancient times, the sixth hour was six hours after sunrise, or high noon. Jesus had been walking all morning and He was exhausted. The sun was shining bright overhead and it was a hot day.

When Jesus sat down at the well, He was tired. He wanted to rest. It was time for a nap. But when He saw the Samaritan woman coming, He knew she needed a touch from God. Her need for truth was greater than His need for rest. Jesus chose to witness instead of sleep.

Many times, God will give you opportunities to witness even when you do not feel like witnessing. You may be tired, busy, or preoccupied. But, you should be willing to witness even when it is inconvenient.

Soul Winners recognize OPPORTUNITIES to witness.

"A woman of Samaria came to draw water..." (John 4:7)

When Jesus saw the Samarian woman, He recognized an opportunity to minister to her. What opportunities do you have to minister to people in your everyday life? Do you recognize the opportunities God gives you?

The little boy from the horror movie "The Sixth Sense" said, "I see dead people. They're everywhere." In a similar way, the master soul winner sees spiritually dead people everywhere he or she looks.

When I look at people through my own eyes, I see a tired business man ready to return home after a long day of flying. I see a busy mother trying to keep control of her toddlers. I see a beggar collecting change to buy a beer. But when I look through the eyes of Jesus, I see lost people who are ready to be saved.

I pray every day that I would see people as Jesus sees them. It is important to keep our eyes open for witnessing opportunities as we go about our daily lives. Recently my wife and I had a garage sale. After an hour of watching people come and go, we realized it was the perfect opportunity to witness. I began giving away copies of my book "Welcome to the Kingdom" that I wrote for new believers. Every family that drove up, whether they bought any of our stuff or not, received a free book and prayer. Half the people who came were Hispanic and I found they were very receptive to the Gospel as soon as they discovered I speak Spanish. At the end of the day, the garage sale made a $267 profit and gave us the opportunity to minister to dozens of people. Two people were saved on the spot!

Every person has a sphere of influence. You encounter people everyday that your pastor never gets a chance to meet. For many people in your circle you may be the ONLY person that God has in their lives with an opportunity to witness to them. If you do not recognize your opportunity to minister to them, perhaps no one else ever will.

Do you look for divine opportunities to witness? Who do you know that needs spiritual help? Where do you go that your pastor never goes? Do you ever think about praying for someone at the grocery store? When was the last time you asked someone if they are saved?

6

Soul Winners TARGET THE LOST with their prayer and witnessing.

Who do you know that needs Jesus? I want you to stop reading right now and find a pen. Write down the names of seven people in your life who are pre-believers. These may be family members, next-door neighbors, co-workers, friends or casual acquaintances.

My Seven for Heaven List:

Name	Today's Date	Date Saved
1._____	_____	_____
2._____	_____	_____
3._____	_____	_____
4._____	_____	_____
5._____	_____	_____
6._____	_____	_____
7._____	_____	_____

I want you to commit to pray for each of these people every day for thirty days. Reach out to each one in a tangible way over the next month. Call them. Invite them to church. Write them a letter. E-mail them. Text message them. Do something to present the Gospel to each person on your list.

At our international crusades, we ask every believer in the city to target seven unsaved individuals for prayer. After thirty days of prayer, the believer invites each of the people on his list to the crusade. Most of the people who get saved at our crusades came because of a personal invitation from a local believer.

Every church member should get involved in leading the lost to Christ. I encourage churches to periodically devote a Sunday specifically to soul winning. Ask everyone in the church to bring at least one person who needs Jesus. The pastor targets his message at presenting the Gospel and then gives an altar call. Immediately, the church offers discipleship classes for the new believers.

Soul Winners ENGAGE people in conversations.

"...Jesus said to her, "Give Me a drink." (John 4:7)

Jesus started a conversation with the Samaritan woman. Asking for a drink was a perfectly natural way to begin talking with her. Often, the first step to leading a stranger to Christ is simply to begin a conversation. How can you lead a stranger to Christ unless you talk to him or her? Normal everyday conversations can be doorways to ministry.

Are you introverted or extroverted? Is it easy for you to talk to a stranger or is it difficult? Regardless, God can use your personality to lead people to Jesus. I have always been introverted. If I have a choice between talking to someone or being by myself I prefer to stay in my cave alone. I have always admired people who are the "life of the party." Some people easily make new friends and talk to total strangers without a moment's hesitation. But, even though I am not naturally gifted when it comes to talking to random strangers, I have developed the skill.

My wife Jessica amazes me. She approaches random strangers and says, "That's a beautiful blouse you're wearing. Where did you buy it?" Within ten seconds she has made a new friend and is discussing sales throughout the mall.

Be friendly with people. One key to leading people to Jesus is to care about them as individuals. Someone once said, "No one cares how much you know, until they know how much you care." Ask people questions about their kids, their pets, their clothes, their situation. Strike up conversations and you will be amazed how many new friends you will make. Once someone is your friend, they will be open to hearing the Gospel.

Soul winners should build a bridge of friendship and strive to find common ground with those they meet. Initiate relationships. Spend time with others. Gather around similar interests or common experiences. If you open your mouth and start a conversation then God will open a door for you to lead someone to Christ.

You may not be able to save everyone, but you can share your faith with someone. I began talking to a teenager behind the counter at a gas station. After we chatted about the weather and how many customers come into the store, I asked him a simple question, "Do you know for sure you are going to heaven?"

He replied, "I think so."

I said, "You can know so." God's word says that you can be sure whether you are going to heaven. "He who has Jesus has life; he who does not have Jesus does not have life" (1 John 5:12).

"Have you made Jesus the Lord of your life?"

"No," he said.

"Would you like to?"

"Yes."

"Repeat this prayer after me. Dear God in heaven, I make Jesus the Lord of my life. I pledge to serve Him all the days of my life. I believe Jesus died for my sins. I have eternal life. In the Name of Jesus, amen." It was that easy to lead the teenager to Jesus.

8

Soul Winners refuse to make EXCUSES for not witnessing.

"For His disciples had gone away into the city to buy food. Then the woman of Samaria said to Him, "How is it that You, being a Jew, ask a drink from me, a Samaritan woman?" For Jews have no dealings with Samaritans." (John 4:8-9)

There are many reasons Jesus should not have spoken to this woman. If Jesus had wanted to make an excuse not to speak to her, it would have been very easy for Him to do so.

1. She was a Samaritan. Jews were known for hating Samaritans. They avoided speaking to them or interacting with them. Jews thought Samaritan people were unclean and they feared that they themselves would become unclean by speaking with them.

2. She was a woman. Jewish men did not speak indiscriminately to woman.

3. She was of ill-repute. Later on in the story, we find that she is a divorcée and an adulterer. She would not have been at the well alone in the middle of the day if she were an upstanding woman in her community.

The disciples headed into the town to buy food and they probably passed this woman trudging towards the well. None of the twelve disciples stopped and spoke to this woman. Each of them probably had a perfectly valid excuse for not speaking to her, but Jesus ignored all the excuses and reached out. All they saw was one of the hated Samaritan women, but Jesus saw her and knew she was lost.

Jesus did not judge her; He reached out to her. Jesus did not condemn her. He did not say, "You must be one of those sinful Samaritan women!" Jesus did not ignore the woman. He did not insult the woman. He did not glare at her for interrupting His rest. Instead, He engaged her in a friendly conversation.

Excuses that STOP people from Soul Winning

Here are some common excuses that prevent believers from reaching out to the lost:

* I am too busy. I don't have time. I'm too tired.
* I don't know what to say. I might say the wrong thing.
* I don't want to offend anyone. I'm scared of what people will think about me. I don't want people to think I am a fanatic.
* I am afraid of rejection. They might laugh at me…beat me up…put me down, etc.
* I don't talk to that kind of person. I don't want to witness to a person who looks different, smells weird, acts strange, or comes from a foreign culture.
* It's not my calling. It's not my job. It's the job of the evangelist.
* I'm called to pray for the lost, not actually talk to them.
* I don't have money to go on a mission trip.
* I'm the wrong age. I'm too old. I'm too young.
* I've not been led by the Holy Spirit. I don't talk to anyone

unless God tells me to.
* I don't care for the lost. I'm more concerned with my family. I don't want to be bothered by talking to strangers.
* In my country you can be killed for trying to convert someone.
* My workplace forbids me to witness. I'll lose business if I try to minister to my customers.

None of these excuses should stop us from witnessing. Jesus had many excuses not to witness to the Samaritan woman, but He ignored the excuses and reached out to her anyway.

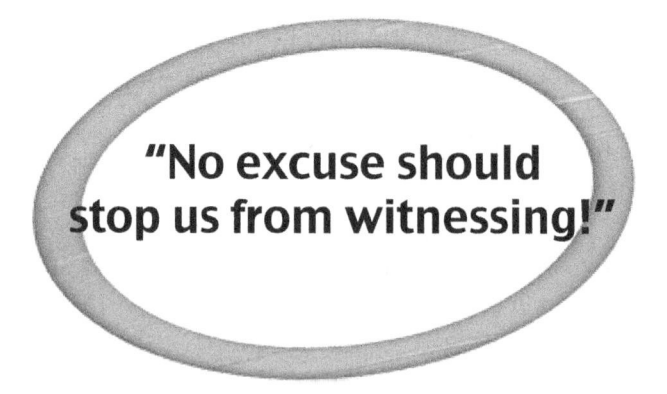

"No excuse should stop us from witnessing!"

9

Soul Winners talk with those who are DIFFERENT.

Everyone has a comfort zone. Your circle may include friends and family you spend a lot of time with. Perhaps you are most comfortable with people in your same profession. Or those within your particular racial or social group. But the master soul winner moves outside his or her circle of comfort to reach out to people who are different and unfamiliar.

We must be willing to leave our own kind and minister to those who are different than us. In Acts 1:8, we find four areas the disciples are commanded to be a witness to: Jerusalem, Judea, Samaria, and the uttermost ends of the earth. How do these circles relate to you?

Jerusalem was the city the disciples lived in. Most of the people in Jerusalem were Jews who came from the same cultural background as the disciples and spoke the same language. So, your Jerusalem would be people who live in your city that are like you in most aspects.

Judea was like the state or country the disciples lived in. It was near where they lived, with a similar culture as theirs. The modern equivalent of ministering in Judea would be me going from Oklahoma to minister to people in Texas or Canada.

Samaria was a nearby area that had a radically different culture than the Jewish culture. Your modern-day Samaria would be going to Mexico on a mission trip or ministering to native-Americans, or even to Asians, Muslims, Indians, Russians, or Hispanics who live near you. So, ministering in Samaria is ministering to those who live near you but have a substantially different culture than you do. Since we have so many sub-cultures within society today, this group could also include: homosexuals, the MTV generation, businessmen and women, the homeless, gangsters, children, politicians, youth, college students, Goths, etc. Your Samaria may even include those who simply have a different focus in life than you do, perhaps your Samaria is reaching out to someone who likes golfing, fishing, hunting, motorcycles, stamp collecting, quilting, etc.

The ends of the earth are those who live far away and have a different culture than you. When we go to India to minister to Hindu people, I feel like we are at the ends of the earth. Did you ever notice that the earth is a circular shape? Where is the end of a circle? There is no end. When Jesus said to "go to the ends of the earth," He meant we should go everywhere and tell everyone about Jesus!

We should be prepared to minister within our own culture and in other cultures, both near and far. As my wife and I have traveled and led people to Christ in over fifty nations around the world, we have discovered that the Gospel works the same no matter where you are or to whom you are speaking with. In every culture, religion, language group, ethnic group, social class, or educational level, there are people ready to receive Jesus as their Savior from sin.

10

Soul Winners leave their COMFORT ZONE and reach into other people's worlds.

Once when I was a teenager, my father asked me to care for my four-year-old brother David. I was reading an exciting novel, so I tried to get my brother to sit down and be quiet while I read. When my father checked up on me, he was upset. He said, "Daniel, when I ask you to baby-sit, I expect you to get down into David's world and play with him." Instead of trying to get my brother to enter my world of reading, I was supposed to get into his world and play with toy trucks.

Sometimes we try to do the same thing when we are soul winning. We expect others to enter our world, i.e. come to church. Instead, we should enter their world and minister to them where they are. Once they grow up spiritually, they can enter our world, but when we are trying to reach them, we must enter the world they live in.

The master soul winner tries to meet people where they are. She gets into their world. Jesus talked to the Samaritan woman on her own level. He got into her world. She was coming to the well to get water, so He asked her for a drink. Nothing could be simpler.

We all have a "comfort zone" where we feel comfortable talking to people who are similar to us. But, if we are truly going to reach the world, we must be willing to step outside of our "comfort zone" and talk to those who are different.

My friend Merritt Hunt explained his method of soul winning to me. He calls this "The Columbo Approach" named after the TV detective who would ask innocent questions until he suddenly solved the crime. Success books say the best way for you to get someone interested in you, is to be interested in them. One effective question for opening up a conversation is to ask someone, "What do you do for a living?" After you listen to them for a while, they may ask you, "Well, what do you do for a living?"

If you are a financial planner, you might say, "I do investments, but that's not what I am really excited about." Then just stop talking for a second. This gets their curiosity aroused and they ask, "What are you really excited about?"

You reply, "I am excited about helping people get to heaven. By the way, do you know how to get to heaven?"

My friend's method is effective because he starts by asking them what they do, instead of talking about himself. He enters their world, before he asks them to enter his. If you will leave your world and enter the world of another, you will discover opportunities for sharing the Gospel.

Soul Winners turn the CONVERSATION towards God.

"Jesus answered and said to her, "If you knew the gift of God, and who it is who says to you, "Give Me a drink," you would have asked Him, and He would have given you living water."

The woman said to Him, "Sir, You have nothing to draw with, and the well is deep. Where then do You get that living water? Are You greater than our father Jacob, who gave us the well, and drank from it himself, as well as his sons and his livestock?"

Jesus answered and said to her, "Whoever drinks of this water will thirst again, but whoever drinks of the water that I shall give him will never thirst. But the water that I shall give him will become in him a fountain of water springing up into everlasting life." (John 4:10-14)

Jesus very quickly turned His conversation towards eternal truth. Instead of gossiping about the weather, or a sports game, or the political situation, He brought up a spiritual topic.

I was eating lunch in the Minneapolis airport when a man came and sat next to me. As he sat down he said, "Thank God for this food." Then he stood back up, "Praise God, I forgot the mustard." When he returned he said, "Hallelujah, it is a beautiful day." Then he turned to me and said, "Excuse me, do you mind if I pray over my food?" Before I could respond he had bowed his head and was praying, "Thank You, God, for being so good to me!" Then he asked me, "Is there anything you need prayer for?" By the time we finished our conversation I was thinking, "If I was lost, I would either run away from this guy as fast as I can or I would fall to my knees and cry out to God for forgiveness."

As a soul winner, I try to keep my eyes open for opportunities to witness to people. Recently, I was sitting on a plane and a man asked me, "Sir, is this seat saved?" I replied, "No, but I can tell you how you can be saved." I took the opportunity to turn the conversation towards God.

Another man asked me, "Man, do you have a light?" I replied, "Yes! I have a Light, let me tell you about Him." All the man wanted was a cigarette, but what he needed was Jesus.

If someone tells you, "I'm lost, can you give me directions?" why don't you say, "If you are lost, I can give you directions to heaven."

If you are at the grocery story, and the clerk asks, "Do you want paper or plastic?" you can reply, "Do you want to go to heaven or Hell?"

Whatever is in you will come out of you. When a balloon pops, air comes out. When a water pipe leaks, water comes out. If you are full of God's word, when you begin speaking to someone who has needs, God's word will pour out of you. After you have initiated a conversation, turn the conversation towards the things of God.

12

Soul Winners tap into their SPIRITUAL GIFTING.

"The woman said to Him, "Sir, give me this water, that I may not thirst, nor come here to draw." Jesus said to her, "Go, call your husband, and come here." The woman answered and said, "I have no husband." Jesus said to her, "You have well said, "I have no husband," for you have had five husbands, and the one whom you now have is not your husband; in that you spoke truly." The woman said to Him, "Sir, I perceive that You are a prophet…" (John 4:15-19)

Jesus discerned her spiritual condition and used His prophetic gift to speak into her life. The Bible talks about a variety of spiritual gifts. Some are called to be prophets, others pastors or teachers or evangelists or apostles. Some have a gift of discernment, gifts of healing, a gift of prophecy, or a gift of encouragement. Jesus operated in all the spiritual gifts and in this story we see Him using the gift of the "word of knowledge."

Jesus already knew she had problems because she came to the well alone. Normally, all the women would go to the well together, just like women today all head to the bathroom in flocks. During the cool of the evening the village women would walk to the well chatting together about the day's events. But this woman came alone during the hottest part of the day.

The Samaritan woman had five husbands and the man she was living with was not her husband. She had probably stolen husbands from the other women in the village and because of this she was rejected by society. She was known as a hussy. One preacher has called her, "The whore in John chapter four."

When I am witnessing, I keep one ear tuned to the voice of God. One word from God can completely turn a conversation around and open up hearts and minds. Someone can be totally antagonistic to the Gospel, but one divine insight into what they are facing can soften their hearts. Every person on earth has a need and if God reveals that need to me, it gives me an enormous advantage in the conversation. So while I am in the middle of a conversation, I listen to what the Holy Spirit is saying.

Recently, I was witnessing to a man and felt an impression to ask him, "How is your wife?" The man immediately broke down and tears came to his eyes. He told me his marriage was falling apart and his wife was about to divorce him. Because he was hurting he became very open for me to pray with him. How did I know to ask him about his wife? I did not hear the audible voice of God telling me he was having marriage problems, but I did feel an impression that was the Holy Spirit inside of me giving a clue about how to minister to him.

Often when I am speaking to someone, God gives me a word of knowledge about what condition they are facing. I ask, "Are you suffering from back pain? Headaches? Do you need a financial miracle? Have you been questioning if God is real?"

When you are witnessing to a sinner, begin listening to the voice of God. Perhaps God will tell you, "Ask how her marriage is going." Or you might feel an impression to pray for financial blessing for the person you are witnessing to. God may give you a word of knowledge and tell you to pray for healing for the person's knees.

You have a spiritual gifting, and if you will be sensitive to the Spirit of God, you will be able to tap into your spiritual gift and use it as a tool to lead people to Jesus.

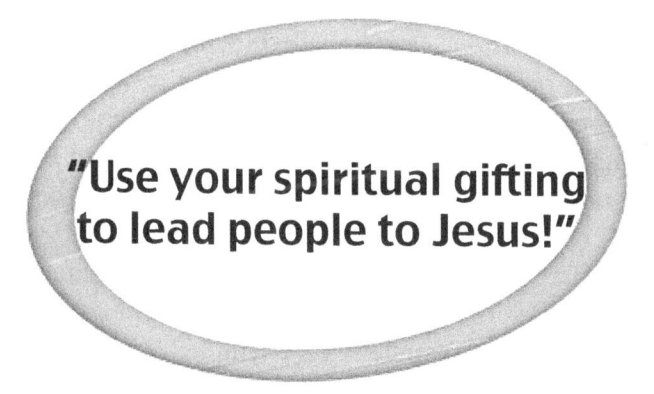

"Use your spiritual gifting to lead people to Jesus!"

Soul Winners ignore attempts to start a spiritual ARGUMENT.

"...Our fathers worshiped on this mountain, and you Jews say that in Jerusalem is the place where one ought to worship."

Jesus said to her, "Woman, believe Me, the hour is coming when you will neither on this mountain, nor in Jerusalem, worship the Father. You worship what you do not know; we know what we worship, for salvation is of the Jews. But the hour is coming, and now is, when the true worshipers will worship the Father in spirit and truth; for the Father is seeking such to worship Him. God is Spirit, and those who worship Him must worship in spirit and truth." (John 4:20-24)

The Samaritan woman tried to start an argument with Jesus. She pointed out, "We worship at this mountain, but Jews say you must worship at the temple." This was a long-standing controversy between the Jews and the Samaritans.

The Samaritans were descendants of Jacob from the ten tribes that had rebelled during the time of Rehoboam. But they had mixed with other races during the Babylonian captivity (2 Kings 17:24). Because of their mixed ancestry, there was great animosity between the Jews and the Samaritans.

Any of the rabbis could have given the Samaritan woman a hundred reasons why she was wrong, but Jesus basically ignored her spiritual notions. He listened, but He did not get offended. He did not argue with her. Instead, He continued to focus on the truth.

Everyone thinks some random thing about spiritual life. It is absolutely amazing to me what ridiculous beliefs people try to share with you. One man told me that UFO's are coming to kidnap us. One woman started talking about healing crystals. Some people say that they are god. Others say nature is god. Atheists will tell you there is no god. A man told me the Mayan calendar signifies the end of the world is about to arrive. Muslims will tell you that Allah is God and Mohammed is his prophet. Hindus will tell you there are many gods. Buddhists say they meditate to become one with the universe. A woman told me her pets would help her get to heaven. Another told me that magnets could cure any disease.

When people bring up controversies about spiritual junk, do not fall into the trap of arguing how they are wrong. When we witness, our goal is not to win arguments, but to win souls. How many arguments do you have to win for someone to fall in love with you? It is a waste of time to argue. If you get them saved, God will take care of the rest of the issues they face.

If someone starts sharing his belief system with me, I politely listen. As I am listening, I silently pray for God to give me wisdom to answer them. By listening, I show that I care for them as an individual. But, no matter how outrageous their claims, I just go back to what the Bible says.

When I speak with people from different religions, I try not to get in a religious argument with them. In the past, I made the mistake of arguing with people over their religion but our conversations never went anywhere.

But now, if I talk to a Jewish person I start by thanking him. I say, "Wow, you are Jewish? I am so thankful for the Jews because without you I would not be here. Everything Gentiles know about God comes from the Jews. My Savior was a Jew. All the preachers of the early church were Jews. I love the Jews."

I take a similar approach when speaking with Muslims. I begin by talking about how much the Koran talks about Jesus. Islam recognizes that Jesus was a prophet, born of a virgin mother, that Jesus does miracles, and that he is coming again to judge the living and the dead. Some churches have stopped preaching the virgin birth, so I actually have a lot in common with Muslims. This serves as a starting point to tell them about Jesus.

If I speak to a Hindu man, I begin by complimenting his religion, "Hindus are such deep spiritual people. I have studied your religion and it is obvious that you have a great hunger for God." With Buddhists, I talk about what a great spiritual leader Buddha was. With atheists, I compliment them for being intellectual skeptics and for their courage to ask questions.

When people share their spiritual notions with you, listen, but do not argue. Just keep going back to the truth of God's word.

Common Objections and Biblical Answers

It is human nature to make excuses and to justify sin. The tendency to make excuses goes all the way back to the first man Adam. After he sinned he told God, "The woman whom You gave to be with me, she gave me of the tree, and I ate" (Genesis 3:12). In one sentence, he blamed his wife and God for the sin that he committed. People today make excuses too.

Here are some common reasons people give for not becoming a Christian and some verses that will help you answer their objections. No matter what people say to you, just keep answering them with the truth of God's word.

I'll become a Christian someday, but not now. "Behold, now is the accepted time; behold, now is the day of salvation" (2 Corinthians 6:2). If you were to die tonight, would you go to heaven? No one is promised tomorrow. It would be a great tragedy for you to die without getting right with God.

Everyone in the church is a hypocrite. "Peter, seeing him, said to Jesus, But Lord, what about this man? Jesus said to him, If I will that he remain till I come, what is that to you? You follow Me" (John 21:21-22). Everyone in the church may be a hypocrite, but we always have room for one more. You might as well come join our church.

I don't believe there is a hell. "And being in torments in Hades, he lifted up his eyes and saw Abraham afar off, and Lazarus in his bosom. Then he cried and said, Father Abraham, have mercy on me, and send Lazarus that he may dip the tip of his finger in water and cool my tongue; for I am tormented in this flame. But Abraham said, Son, remember that in your lifetime you received your good things, and likewise Lazarus evil things; but now he is comforted and you are tormented. And besides all this, between us and you there is a great gulf fixed, so that those who want to pass from here to you cannot, nor can those from there pass to us" (Luke 16:23-26). Truth is truth regardless of whether you believe it or not. There is a heaven, and a hell. You must choose where you will spend eternity.

I have to give up all my fun if I become a Christian. "But when he came to himself, he said, How many of my father's hired servants have bread enough and to spare, and I perish with hunger!" (Luke 15:17) Life with God is always better than life without God. You may feel like you are having fun drinking and partying, but ultimately, the price for sin is death and destruction. When Jesus comes to live in your heart, you will have more peace, more joy, more blessing than you can imagine.

I do not believe in the Bible. "For assuredly, I say to you, till heaven and earth pass away, one jot or one tittle will by no means pass from the law till all is fulfilled" (Matthew 5:18). The Bible is the greatest selling book in history. Millions of lives have been changed after reading the Bible. All the prophecies of the Old Testament are perfectly fulfilled in the New Testament. I know the Bible is true because it has changed my life.

I am not good enough to be a Christian. "And I give them eternal life, and they shall never perish; neither shall anyone snatch them out of My hand. My Father, who has given them to Me, is greater than all; and no one is able to snatch them out of My Father's hand." (John 10:28-29) No one is good enough to be a Christian. We all need God's forgiveness. You do not have to be good; all you have to do is trust Jesus for your salvation.

I have committed far too many sins for God to accept me. "If we confess our sins, He is faithful and just to forgive us our sins and to cleanse us from all unrighteousness" (1 John 1:9). No matter what sin you have committed in your past, you can have a wonderful future with Jesus Christ. Jesus died on the cross to pay the price for all of your sins.

God is too good to send anyone to hell. "As I live, says the Lord GOD, I have no pleasure in the death of the wicked, but that the wicked turn from his way and live. Turn, turn from your evil ways!" (Ezekiel 33:11) God is a good God, but He is also a holy God. He cannot allow sin to enter heaven lest all of heaven be corrupted. Hell was created for the devil and his evil angels. God does not want you to go to hell. God, out of his goodness, sent me to talk to you today. If you respond to His goodness, you do not have to go to hell.

I live a good life. God will let me into heaven because I am such a good person. "…for all have sinned and fall short of the glory of God" (Romans 3:23). No matter how good you are, you are not good enough to meet God's standards. Imagine trying to jump across the Grand Canyon. If you were an Olympic long jumper and jumped as far as you possibly could, you would end up in the same place as an overweight man trying to jump the canyon. It is impossible for us to be good enough through our own efforts to get to heaven.

I don't feel like becoming a Christian. "Behold, I stand at the door and knock. If anyone hears My voice and opens the door, I will come in to him and dine with him, and he with Me" (Revelation 3:20). God is calling your name right now. Will you answer His call?

There are many ways to get to heaven. "Jesus said to him, I am the way, the truth, and the life. No one comes to the Father except through Me" (John 14:6). Only Jesus can save you. Many religious leaders have tried to reveal the way to get to heaven, but they all died. Jesus is the only one who rose from the dead to show us the way to get to God.

There is no God. "The fool has said in his heart, "There is no God." (Psalm 14:1). One philosopher said, "God is dead," but now God is saying, "That philosopher is dead." You may not believe in God, but God believes in you. He believes in you so much that He sent me to talk to you today.

I might be saved, but I'm not sure? "We know that we have passed from death to life" (1 John 3:14). You can have an assurance of salvation. You can know that you are saved. If someone says, "I don't know if I am saved," this is like saying "I don't know if I am married." You don't think you are married, you don't try to be married, either you are or you are not. God's word promises, "Whoever calls on the name of the Lord shall be saved" (Acts 2:21). Notice this verse promises that if you call on Jesus, you "shall be" saved, not "might be" saved or "possibly be" saved.

Handle spiritual objections that people raise by going back to God's word. Be like Jesus, do not get in an argument, just keep speaking the truth.

Soul Winners REVEAL JESUS to the hurting.

"The woman said to Him, "I know that Messiah is coming" (who is called Christ). When He comes, He will tell us all things." Jesus said to her, "I who speak to you am He." (John 4:25-26)

Jesus revealed Himself to the Samaritan woman. Ultimately, the reason people get saved is because they see who Jesus really is. It is our job to reveal Jesus to the lost. Jesus said, "if I am lifted up from the earth, I will draw all peoples to Myself" (John 12:32).

Jesus is the answer to the world's problems. The more people know about Jesus, the more likely they are to become a follower of Christ. The Samaritan woman was looking for answers to her spiritual problems and Jesus revealed that He is the answer.

As soul winners, our job is to point people to Jesus. It is Jesus that draws mankind to the Father. Jesus is the stumbling block. Either you accept Him or you do not. He is the line that divides history. He is the One everyone must confront: to accept or deny. Is He just a prophet or the Messiah? As C.S. Lewis asked, "Is He liar, lunatic, or Lord?" Ultimately, Christianity rises and falls on the person of Christ.

In our international soul winning festivals, we do not waste time talking negatively about other religions. We never preach against Mohammad, Buddha, or Hinduism. Instead, we preach about Who Jesus is and what He accomplished on the cross. It's all about Jesus!

When I preach to the lost, I begin by telling stories of what Jesus did in the New Testament, then I tell stories about the miracles Jesus has done in the lives of others. Finally I share about what Jesus has done in my own life. The people hear how Jesus saves, heals and delivers. By the time I am finished preaching, Jesus is irresistible.

When Jesus is revealed, people get saved. The more people learn about Jesus, the more likely they are to become a Christian. Our assignment is to reveal Jesus. It is not our responsibility to bring all people to Christ, but to bring Christ to all people.

The world is salvation hungry and salvation willing. It is not that the world is unwilling to be believers; it is that they have not heard. Most people have not rejected the Gospel; they just have not heard the Gospel. Perhaps they have been exposed to dead religion their whole lives, perhaps a hypocritical believer was mean to them, perhaps no one has ever compassionately shared the Gospel with them. I am convinced that when the right person shares the right word at the right time, Jesus is irresistible. Many people are ready and waiting to receive Jesus, all they are waiting for is you to invite them to heaven.

Jesus is the key to evangelism. The reason more people do not accept Christ is because many of them do not know who He is. So, when you are witnessing, reveal Jesus to people.

15

Soul Winners know that the NEWLY SAVED are the best evangelists.

"And at this point His disciples came, and they marveled that He talked with a woman; yet no one said, "What do You seek?" or, "Why are You talking with her?" The woman then left her waterpot, went her way into the city, and said to the men, "Come, see a Man who told me all things that I ever did. Could this be the Christ?" Then they went out of the city and came to Him" (John 4:27-30).

The Samaritan woman became a better evangelist than the disciples. Everyone from the town came to see Jesus because of her testimony. Her testimony did more in five minutes than twelve professional preachers accomplished the whole time they were buying food.

As soon as a sinner gets saved, we should turn him or her into an evangelist. Once one person in a family gets on fire for God, it does not take long for the rest of the family to turn to Jesus. Today's SOUL SAVED is tomorrow's SOUL WINNER!

Soul Winners know that every person can make a DIFFERENCE.

One night thousands of starfish washed up on a sandy beach. The next morning, a little boy noticed the starfish drying up and dying as the water receded. He began running up and down the beach picking up starfish and throwing them back into the ocean.

An old man watched from his house porch. He called out to the boy, "Son, there are thousands of starfish dying. Even if you worked all day long, you would not be able to rescue all the starfish. You are not making any difference."

The boy looked at the old man, then he reached down and picked up one starfish. He said, "I may not be able to save all the starfish, but I can make a difference in the life of this one." Then he threw the starfish back into the water.

You may not be able to save everyone in your city, but you can save someone. You may not be able to lead everyone to Christ, but you can make sure that those you do meet have an opportunity to spend eternity in heaven.

Soul Winners realize that soul winning is the most IMPORTANT activity on earth.

"In the meantime His disciples urged Him, saying, "Rabbi, eat." But He said to them, "I have food to eat of which you do not know." Therefore the disciples said to one another, "Has anyone brought Him anything to eat?" Jesus said to them, "My food is to do the will of Him who sent Me, and to finish His work"
(John 4:31-34).

For Jesus, witnessing to the Samaritan woman was more important than eating. Jesus placed more importance on her eternal destiny than He did on His own physical needs. This is a good lesson for us in today's busy world. We race from work, to shopping, to soccer practice, to a PTA meeting, and then home for must-see-TV. In the midst of all this busyness it is hard to take the time to actually talk to someone about God.

Soul winning is the only activity that will matter 10,000 years from now. Soul winning is the only investment that will bear eternal dividends. Soul winning is the single most important activity you can engage in.

Jesus tells His disciples that His number one priority (even more important than eating) is obeying the will of His Father. Jesus witnessed to the Samaritan woman, because He knew His Father's heart.

God's heartbeat is for people. If you listened to God's heartbeat with a stethoscope, you would hear it say, "People, people, people, people." We put together a great music video about the heartbeat of God. Check it out on my website: www.kingministries.com.

Right now, feel your pulse with your finger. When you feel your heartbeat, I want you to think of God's heartbeat.

Now, stand up and do ten jumping jacks. Feel your pulse again. What happened? Your heartbeat sped up, right? Why? Because you began to move. Do you want to see more people get saved? If you do, you need to begin to move!

When you move, God moves. You are God's hands. You are God's feet. You are God's voice to this world. The only Jesus some people will ever see is you. We reveal Jesus to people through our words and our actions.

God could send 10,000 angels, but He chose to use us. We are His instruments here on earth. Lift up your hands and say this out loud, "My hands are healing hands. Every person I touch feels the healing touch of Jesus."

Now, place your hands on your mouth and say, "My voice is a Gospel voice. Every word I speak brings people closer to God."

Finally, touch your feet and say, "My feet are beautiful feet. God's word says, 'Beautiful are the feet of them who bring good news.' Everywhere I go, I bring good news about Jesus Christ."

I believe Jesus is coming soon. Because of His imminent return, God is speeding up what is happening on the earth today. Recently someone asked me, "Daniel, how is it that someone at your young age can reach so many people?" It is not because I am special. It is simply because as Christ's return draws closer, God is speeding up the harvest time. What used to take ten years, now takes one. What used to take a lifetime can now be accomplished in a few months.

The greatest harvest of souls in history will occur in the next few years. Because of exploding population growth around the world, more people will become Jesus believers in the next decade than in all of history. This means the church militant here on earth will be bigger than the church triumphant in heaven. More people are alive today than ever before and millions will give their lives to Jesus!

The task that the church has been diligently pursuing for two thousand years is almost done. For centuries, great men and woman of faith have planted and watered and now it time to bring in the harvest. People are hungry for God around the world. There has never been greater interest in the supernatural. This is our opportunity. The harvest is ripe.

Soul Winners know that all of HEAVEN IS WATCHING.

"Jesus said to them, "My food is to do the will of Him who sent Me, and to finish His work" (John 4:34).

Jesus knew God the Father was watching Him. His passion was to finish the job His Father had given Him to do. All of heaven is also watching us as we witness to the lost.

Imagine a huge stadium. In the grandstands are all the great heroes of the Bible. Moses, Joshua, David, Daniel, Esther, Paul, and Peter are watching. Alongside are all the heroes of the church. Tertullian, Clement, Luther, Wesley, Whitefield, Kulhman and Wigglesworth are there. On the track, you are running as fast as you can. You are carrying a baton that has been passed to you by previous generations.

Those in the stands are the "great crowd of witnesses" that the writer of Hebrews tells us about, "Therefore let us also, seeing we are compassed about with so great a cloud of witnesses, lay aside every weight, and the sin which doth so easily beset us, and let us run with patience the race that is set before us" (Hebrews 12:1).

Those in the stands are not sitting down. They are standing on their feet cheering you on. They are shouting, "Go! Go! Go!" The baton has been passed to us. We are standing on the shoulders of spiritual giants. We are privileged to live during this final time of harvest.

What will you do? Will you sit in the church pew like a bump on a log, or will you stand up and take your place in the army of soul winners God is raising up? Will you be satisfied with living a comfortable life, or will you be energized to do great exploits for God?

> "All of heaven is cheering for you as you lead people to Jesus!"

Soul Winners are PASSIONATE about leading the lost to Christ.

How did I become passionate about leading people to Jesus? Several years ago, I went on a mission trip to the country of Jamaica. Our group experienced powerful ministry at churches and evangelistic crusades. Hundreds of people were saved and many miraculous healings were reported. The days in Jamaica were extremely hot and quite humid, so as we walked through neighborhoods inviting people to church, we quickly overheated. By the time we arrived back at our hotel that evening, we were a sticky mess. Unfortunately, the showers at the hotel were broken. We fixed this problem by deciding to go for a late night swim in the pool.

As we swam, I noticed there was a panel near the edge of the pool that looked like it was smoking. I was curious, so I foolishly swam over to check it out. I was treading water beside an underwater light when - zap - I was shocked. The electricity shot through my body and numbed my feet and hands. Terrified, I leapt out of the pool. Immediately, I became concerned for the safety of the other members of my team. I started screaming at them to get out of the pool as fast as they could.

None of them knew what was wrong so they just looked at me. As I kept yelling at them about the danger, some began to get out, but most of the people thought I was playing a practical joke on them so they stayed in the pool. I frantically began grabbing people and pulling them out of the pool. I pointed at the smoking panel and shouted, "Get out!" I yelled repeatedly about the danger until I was hoarse. When everyone realized how serious I was, they climbed out of the pool. Several stubborn boys refused to fall for what they still thought was a practical joke. I was frustrated as I watched them swim in a dangerous situation. I began to talk to them and show them the danger they were in. Finally, my sense of urgency compelled them to climb out of the pool. I was so relieved when I had saved everyone's life!

God stopped me right then and He told me, "You need to save people from hell with the same passion that you saved those people from an electric shock." This word from
God has given me a passion to see the lost saved. By the grace of God, I had been saved from being electrocuted. After I had been spared, I began to yell and scream, and pull people out of danger. I experienced an intense urgency about it. I did not rest until everyone was saved, because I was concerned for their lives.

God revealed to me that I need to be just as concerned about the lives of people who are headed for hell! I have to do whatever it takes to rescue someone from the grasp of Satan. If I have to speak loud and boldly, I will. If I have to talk them into salvation, I will. I made a commitment to myself that day that I would do whatever it takes to help save a soul from hell.

You see, too many of us get saved and walk away thanking God for our salvation, but we forget that there are still thousands of people who are headed for hell. We should be like the Samaritan woman and go tell other people about Jesus. Someone has described the Christian walk as "One starving man who has found food, telling another starving man where he can find food." I experienced salvation, and now my duty is to help save others!

20

The Soul Winner knows he or she is like a FARMER.

"Do you not say, "There are still four months and then comes the harvest? Behold, I say to you, lift up your eyes and look at the fields, for they are already white for harvest! And he who reaps receives wages, and gathers fruit for eternal life, that both he who sows and he who reaps may rejoice together." (John 4:35-36)

It is harvest time! My wife Jessica and I have conducted massive miracle crusades in nations around the world. In every country, people are hungry for salvation. Muslims, Hindus, voodoo witch doctors, and Rastafarians have all given their lives to Jesus. What drives us? When Jesus saw the crowds of people, He had compassion on them. He said to His disciples, "Look, the fields are ready for harvest, but the laborers are few. Pray that the Lord of the harvest would send out laborers into his harvest fields." (Matthew 9:37-38)

Four "L"-ements of the Harvest

1. The LOOK of the Harvest. Jesus told His disciples to look at the harvest. Have you ever looked at the harvest fields of the world? When I look at the harvest fields, I see a young Hindu girl starving in India. I see an elderly Muslim man praying to Allah facing Mecca. I see an American family shopping at Wal Mart. I see children in Mexico happily playing soccer. I see an African man herding his precious cows. I see a Buddhist monk chanting and burning incense. I see a stoic soldier of North Korea guarding the DMZ. I have seen all these people with my own eyes. What do you see when you look at the harvest? Lift up your eyes; the fields are ripe for harvest. Look with the eyes of Jesus.

2. The LORD of the Harvest. God the Father is the Lord of the Harvest and He places no limits on the harvest. He wants ALL men to be saved; He promises to pour out His Spirit on ALL flesh; He wants us to go into ALL the world. God's heartbeat is for souls. Oh, that our hearts would beat with the same cadence!

3. The LABORERS of the Harvest. The harvest is ripe, but the workers are few. The threshing machines have rusted, the sickles are lost, and the barn has holes in the roof. The sun is shining, the grain is ready to eat, but the fields are empty of workers. The farmers are still busy with last year's harvest. They are counting, organizing, reporting, and rearranging instead of reaping.

Jesus said the laborers are few. He asks the disciples to pray for laborers to be sent out into the harvest fields (Matthew 9:38). I believe they did pray because in the very next verse (Matthew 10:1) Jesus sends the disciples out as laborers and He gives them authority to do the same miracles

He did. The disciples became the answer to their own prayers! I believe every follower of Jesus is called to work in the harvest fields by praying, giving or going. Go and say, or stay and pray, or help pay the way. YOU are a laborer for Jesus.

The church should send its very best workers out as soul winners. When a farmer harvests a crop, he puts aside his best seed to plant the next year. The best seed produces the best harvest. When we give our best to soul winning, God will give us the best possible harvest.

4. The LENGTH of the Harvest. There is only a brief window of time during which the harvest is ripe. We must make use of this valuable time. The harvest will soon be past; only what is done for Christ will last. These are the last days. Jesus is coming soon. Time is short. We must make every second count for God. A passion for souls burns within me. When I think about the millions of lost people who are dying and going to hell, it makes me weep. It is so vital to do whatever we can to win the lost. You are such an important part of what God is doing. When is the Gospel NOT good news? When it arrives too late.

The sand is running out of the hourglass. The end of the day is nearing. The clock is ready to strike. A new time period is coming. Time is disappearing rapidly. The lost opportunities of yesterday are gone forever. Today is disappearing. Tomorrow is full of potential if we will grasp it. We must fill up the kingdom before time runs out.

Soul Winners are NEVER DISCOURAGED when a person is not saved immediately.

"For in this the saying is true: "One sows and another reaps. I sent you to reap that for which you have not labored; others have labored, and you have entered into their labors" (John 4:37-38).

Everywhere we go, we plant seeds. Sometimes we get to reap a harvest and actually lead someone to Jesus. But, even when someone does not get saved immediately, we should never get discouraged. We just keep on planting and watering seeds.

Someone once said, "Do not judge today by the harvest you reap, but by the seeds you sow." If someone rejects you, they are not really rejecting you, they are rejecting your message and the gentle call of the Holy Spirit.

Soul Winners know that their witnessing will produce GREAT FRUIT.

"*And many of the Samaritans of that city believed in Him because of the word of the woman who testified, "He told me all that I ever did"* (John 4:39).

Even long afterwards, this woman must have continued to tell people about her encounter with Jesus. None of the disciples were present to overhear the conversation, so how did the apostle John know enough about it to write the story in his gospel? After Jesus rose from the dead, the Samaritan woman probably became a Christian and her testimony became a favorite story of the early church.

After Jesus ascended into heaven this area of Samaria was fertile soil for the Gospel, probably in large part because of this woman's witness. When Philip the evangelist began to preach in Samaria, a great move of God was ignited. "Then Philip went down to the city of Samaria and preached Christ to them. And the multitudes with one accord heeded the things spoken by Philip, hearing and seeing the miracles which he did. For unclean spirits, crying with a loud voice, came out of many who were possessed; and many who were paralyzed and lame were healed. And there was great joy in that city" (Acts 8:5-8).

The revival was so great that Philip needed help. "Now when the apostles who were at Jerusalem heard that Samaria had received the word of God, they sent Peter and John to them, who, when they had come down, prayed for them that they might receive the Holy Spirit. For as yet He had fallen upon none of them. They had only been baptized in the name of the Lord Jesus. Then they laid hands on them, and they received the Holy Spirit. (Acts 5:14-17).

The entire region of Samaria was impacted. "So when they had testified and preached the word of the Lord, they returned to Jerusalem, preaching the gospel in many villages of the Samaritans" (Acts 5:25).

"Your witnessing will have a BIG impact!"

Soul Winners build a BIG MONUMENT with their labors.

I saw this report in a magazine, "The Washington Monument (169 meters tall) in Washington D.C. was started in 1848 and finished in 1884. It opened to the public in October of 1885. During a recent renovation of the lobby, construction workers found graffiti from the 1800's which had quite a different tone from that usually found today on the sides of buildings and trains. The markings in the lobby of the monument were covered over when it was decorated at the turn of the century. They were found when workers removed marble wainscoting as part of a year-long $500,000 renovation which was recently completed.

"Whoever is the human instrument under God in the conversion of one soul, enacts a monument to his own memory more lofty and enduring than this" reads the inscription which can now be viewed by visitors of the monument. It is signed B.F.B. No one know who that is, or who left the small drawings and 19th century dates on the other walls.

It is true. Winning one soul to Christ is a much greater monument than anything you can build here on earth. Soul winning is the only investment of time or money that will matter ten thousand years from now.

Charles Spurgeon, the great preacher, said, "'He that winneth souls is wise,' because he has selected a wise object. I think it was Michelangelo who once carved certain magnificent statues in snow. They are gone; the material readily compacted by the frost as readily melted in the heat. Far wiser was he when he fashioned the enduring marble, and produced works which will last all through the ages. But even marble itself is consumed and fretted by the tooth of time; and he is wise who selects for his raw material immortal souls, whose existence shall outlast the stars."

24

Soul Winners aim to "SAVE THE MAN!"

On May 29, 1953 Edmond Hillary became the first human in history to reach the peak of Mount Everest, the tallest mountain in the world. His achievement is one of the greatest accomplishments of mankind.

Controversy erupted recently over others who dreamed of conquering the summit. In May of 2006, climbers who wanted to reach the top passed a mountaineer who was dying on the trail. Instead of stopping to save his life, they chose to pass him by so their dreams would be fulfilled. An old man now, Sir Edmond Hillary was asked what he would have done in the same situation. He replied forcefully, "Save the man!"

When Peter, James, and John wanted to stay on the Mount of Transfiguration, Jesus knew there was a demon-possessed boy who was waiting to be healed. Jesus left the mountaintop to go "save the man!"

This is why we are soul winners. Our goal is to "save the man!"

Soul Winners FOLLOW UP on the fruit.

"So when the Samaritans had come to Him, they urged Him to stay with them; and He stayed there two days. And many more believed because of His own word" (John 4:40-41).

Jesus stayed in the village for two days because He knew the importance of follow-up. Once we catch the fish, we must clean the fish. Once a soul is SAVED, a disciple must be MADE. After a person is saved, satan immediately comes to try to steal the word that was planted. Far too often, spiritual babes are spiritually aborted before they can become mature believers. How can we effectively follow up on new believers?

One of the greatest soul winners I know is Pastor Phillip Goudeaux. His whole church is excited about soul winning, because he himself is a soul winner. As a young man he was a member of the Black Panthers. Once he got saved, he immediately started leading people to Jesus. Today, he pastors a church of over 22,000 people in Sacramento, California. He personally led many of the people in his congregation to Jesus.

Recently, we spoke at a Soul Winning Conference in his church. Afterwards, Pastor Goudeaux said the conference was the best his church had ever hosted. Each morning we did workshops on soul winning, and then led people from the church out into the neighborhoods around the church to knock on doors. In five days, we led over three hundred people to Jesus within a three-mile radius of the church.

Many people who went out soul winning with us began receiving miracles in their own lives. One woman who had suffered from tremors in her hands for many years was healed as she went out witnessing. A man who had been trying to find a job for three months decided to spend his time soul winning since he had nothing else to do, as he was leading a man to Christ, he received a phone call offering him a job. One young lady had never led anyone to Christ in her entire life, within six months of the conference; she had personally led over fifty people to Jesus.

One of the lessons I learned from Dr. Goudeaux is that in order for a church to be a soul winning church, the pastor must set an example by being a soul winner. Every week, he challenges his G-12 groups to be soul winners. His church has purchased hundreds of copies of my book Soul Winning: Inspiration for Leading the Lost to Christ. I wrote a tract specifically for his church and his members gave away over 100,000 copies of the tract within just a few months. His entire congregation is motivated and empowered to be soul winners.

Dr. Goudeaux believes "relationship is the key to effective follow up." The goal is to disciple the convert until he or she is a mature follower of Christ. Let me explain the process that Calvary Christian Center in Sacramento, California uses to follow up on new believers.

1. Get their name, phone number, and address. How can you follow up unless you know how to contact the new believer? Give this information to your church so they can send discipleship material in the mail but keep a copy for yourself. Call the newly born again person several times over the next two weeks to find out how they are doing. Build a relationship.

2. Invite the new believer to church. Statistics show that eight out of ten people will go with you to church if invited. If someone gets saved on Saturday, invite her to come to church the next morning. You may offer to give them a ride to church or promise to take her family out to eat after the service (no one is going to turn down food). Often it can be scary to go to church for the first time, but you can help their children get to the right classes and explain what is going on during the service.

3. Get them plugged into a small discipleship group. Calvary uses the G-12 system of cell groups. Everyone in the church is part of a group of twelve people that meets every week. Ultimately, every person in the church should also start their own group of twelve. The way to start your own group is to lead people to Jesus, and then to start discipling them on a weekly basis. This way, you can pour everything God has taught you into other people.

4. Turn the new believers into soul winners themselves. The process of discipleship is not complete until the new believer is able to duplicate himself by leading someone else to Jesus.

In our international soul winning festivals, we use similar methods to follow up on the thousands of people that get saved. As an evangelist, the criticism I hear the most often is in the area of follow-up. Anytime someone criticizes us for not doing more follow-up, I am reminded of a story about the great evangelist D.L. Moody. One day a lady criticized D. L. Moody for his methods of evangelism in attempting to win people to the Lord. Moody's reply was: "I agree with you. I don't like the way I do it either. Tell me, how do you do it?" The lady replied, "I don't do it." Moody responded, "Well, I like my way of doing it better than your way of not doing it."

At each event we conduct, thousands of decision cards are filled out by new believers and local churches begin to systematically disciple everyone who got saved. We do everything we possibly can to ensure that converts become disciples.

1. Literature distribution. We have spent thousands of dollars printing over 100,000 books, tracks, bibles, or Bible portions to give away to new believers. I am a big believer in the power of the printed page. A book can go farther than I can go, stay longer than I can stay, and can reach far more people than I can personally speak to face-to-face. Books are powerful. God sent His Son for a season, but left His book for eternity. In a Muslim nation recently, we teamed up with another ministry who agreed to send a Bible correspondence course to every new believer who filled out a card. These arrive in the mail in a plain brown envelope in order not to raise the suspicion of neighbors. After ten courses are completed, a New Testament was sent as a gift.

2. Leadership training. We hold leadership conferences for hundreds of pastors and church leaders. Often we spend thousands of dollars to help pay for their transportation, lodging, and meals. Over a three-day period we pour as much knowledge and impartation into them as we can.

3. Home visitation. We train local believers to visit the homes of those who filled out decision cards. This is effective, particularly in Muslim countries, because Muslim culture forbids a Muslim to step foot inside a church, but they are willing to invite a Christian into their house for some tea. At the festival, we announce "If you need prayer for something in your life, please fill out one of the these cards." Muslims are often very anxious to have a Christian come and pray for them because as Muslims in Pakistan told us, "We know that God answers the prayers of the Christians." In Indonesia, we provided money to give a gift of a Bible to everyone who was visited.

4. Operation Andrew. Often, local believers have never led anyone to the Lord or helped anyone grow to spiritual maturity. We often train believers how to be soul winners in the months prior to the festival. In the Bible, Andrew met Jesus, then he ran to bring Peter to Jesus. Using this system developed by Billy Graham, three months before the festival each believer in the city is challenged to write down the names of seven unbelievers. The believer commits to pray for the unbelievers every day. When the festival arrives, the believer goes to each of the seven and invites them to come to the festival. During the festival, the believer often stands with those she invited and is the counselor who prays with them and gives them a book. After the festival, the believer is responsible for inviting them to her church. This works particularly well, especially when we provide buses from different areas. The believer is able to provide a ride, and is able to minister to the new believers on the way to and from the festival grounds. We challenge the churches to fill up the buses with unbelievers, so often a church of thirty will fill up three buses with over one hundred and fifty people.

5. Internet Follow up. Even in third world nations, young people often have e-mail addresses. We collect their e-mail addresses and send them ten weeks of basic discipleship material through e-mail. In Jamaica hundreds of people signed up for our online course.

6. Church Planting. In Pakistan, we paid the salaries of several new pastors for one year after the festival. This gives them time to establish a viable congregation. In Mexico we have constructed church buildings in areas that have no churches.

26

Soul Winners know EVERYONE MUST MEET JESUS for themselves.

"Then they said to the woman, "Now we believe, not because of what you said, for we ourselves have heard Him..." (John 4:42)

The woman witnessed to the village and brought the people to see Jesus, but the people started to follow Jesus because they heard Him for themselves. A common proverb is, "You can lead a horse to water, but you cannot force him to drink." Your testimony can bring someone to Jesus, but they must experience Him for themselves. So, do not get discouraged when your message about Christ is rejected. Do not take it personally. People are not rejecting you, they are rejecting your message. Just keep witnessing as often as you can.

27

Soul Winners know the power of PRINTED MATERIAL.

Even though we do not see Jesus give this woman any printed material, the whole reason we know her story is because the Apostle John wrote it down.

My grandfather was standing on a street corner as a young man. Someone handed him a gospel tract. He read it and got saved. Later he became a missionary to Afghanistan and Saudi Arabia, two of the hardest-to-reach nations in the world. Now, I am a missionary because of his example. The seed of that simple tract has produced a harvest around the world.

I encourage you to keep a stash of gospel literature in your car and in your pocket or purse. Look for opportunities to give tracts to the lost. Print John 3:16 on the back of your business card. Leave a tract along with your tip at a restaurant (makes sure your tip is generous, if you leave a small tip, tell them you are a Jehovah Witness, so you will help in reverse!). Give a tract to the checkout girl at the grocery store. When you go to the bank and send a deposit through the tube, include a tract. Share the Gospel with your dentist. On Halloween, give away some tracts with your candy. Hand a tract to the man behind the counter at the convenience store. One friend of mine unrolls the toilet paper rolls in public bathrooms and rolls it back up with tracts tucked inside the roll (everyone needs reading material when they are sitting there). If a vacuum salesman knocks on your door, send him on his way with a tract.

You are like a farmer sowing seed. Every time you give away a tract, you sow one more Gospel seed. You never know what harvest you will produce.

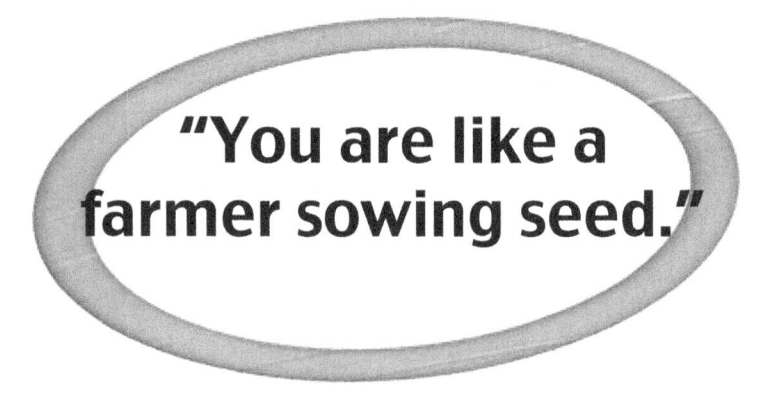

"You are like a farmer sowing seed."

28

Soul Winners know that JESUS IS THE SAVIOR of the World.

"...and we know that this is indeed the Christ, the Savior of the world" (John 4:42).

This was the first time Jesus was revealed as the Savior of the whole world. The disciples suspected Jesus was the anticipated Savior of the Jewish people, but this Samaritan city was the first to realize that Jesus is not just for one race but for all of humanity. What an amazing revelation!

John 3:16 announces the great truth that Jesus came to save the whole world. "For God so loved the world that He gave His only begotten Son, that whoever believes in Him should not perish but have everlasting life." The story of the Samaritan woman confirms this great truth. There is no one in all the world that Jesus cannot save!

29

Soul Winners know they will be HEROES IN HEAVEN.

Imagine your friends gathered together on the porch of your mansion in heaven. You have eaten a scrumptious meal and as the food settles, the group begins to reminisce about the victories won on earth.

"Moses, tell the story again about how God parted the Red Sea," you say.

The great patriarch clears his throat and begins to tell the tale, "There were chariots as far as the eye could see. Pharaoh was shaking his spear in anger. The water loomed up on either side of the passageway through the sea. God's people were quaking in fear. But I lifted up my rod and suddenly the water came tumbling down. Let me tell you, we had a party in the desert that night."

"Daniel, tell us about God saving you from the lions." Breathlessly, you listen as the prophet tells about how an angel shut the mouth of the carnivorous cats.

For hours you ask each other questions.

"Mr. Luther, what were you feeling when you nailed the ninety-five theses up on the door?"

"Noah, was it hard to build a big boat when you had never seen rain?"

"Elijah, were you surprised when fire actually fell from heaven?"

"William Carey, we want to hear about the thousands of heathens saved in India."

"Billy, when you first started preaching, did you ever imagine you would minister to over two hundred million people in your lifetime?"

Suddenly, the party goes silent. A man, with nail scars in his hands, says, "There's one story we haven't heard yet this evening."

A shiver goes up and down your spine. No matter how many times you see Jesus, it's a rush just being in His presence. You wonder which of heaven's heroes Jesus is talking about. Then you realize everyone is looking at you. You glance at Jesus and His finger is pointed in your direction. You look over your shoulder and there is no one behind you.

Jesus says, "My friend, tell us about all the people you witnessed to." With a gulp, you open your mouth and begin.

Each day, you write the story you will tell for eternity. What tale will you tell of today's activities? Are you a master soul winner?

Witnessing Tips

- Have a planned time to go soul winning.
- Be clean and neat. Take breath mints along.
- Be complimentary and gracious.
- Always go door-to-door in groups of two. Jesus sent the disciples out two by two.
- When you witness, one person should do the talking, the other should be praying under their breath.
- Use our Script for Witnessing. Feel free to develop your own.
- Look for opportunities to witness everywhere you go.
- Be bold, loving, humble, and enthusiastic.
- Stay calm, cool, and collected. Don't act crazy, mad, or frustrated.
- Be led by the Holy Spirit.
- The message is more important then the method. Use any way you can to bring Jesus to people.
- Stay away from religious language and terminology. Focus on Jesus.
- Remember, God can save anyone and God can save through anyone, especially through YOU!
- Follow up on each contact and invite them to come to church with you sometime in the next week. Pick them up for church if possible.
- If no one is home, leave a flyer about your church or a gospel tract in the door.

Sample Script for Witnessing

Hello, my name is _____ and this is my friend _____. We are from _____ church. This neighborhood is on our heart and we want to pray for every person and family in this area.

Has anyone ever told you that God loves you and has a wonderful plan for your life? Can we ask you a quick but important question? If you were to die tonight, do you know for sure that you would go to heaven? (If they reply "yes" ask "Why do you say yes"? If they respond with anything but "I have Jesus in my heart" or something similar to that, proceed with the script. If they say "no" or "I hope so" proceed with the script.)

Let me quickly share with you what the Bible says. It reads, "All have sinned and come short of the glory of God" And "the wages of sin is death, but the gift of God is eternal life in Christ Jesus our Lord" It also reads, "Everyone who calls on the name of the Lord shall be saved."

Would you like to call on Jesus right now and make sure that you are saved by saying a short prayer with me? Say this with your heart and with your mouth so you can hear it.

"Dear God in Heaven, I call on Jesus right now to save me. I believe Jesus died on the cross to pay for my sin. I repent of all my sins. I believe Jesus rose from the dead. Right now, I make Jesus the Lord of my life. I want to obey His word. Thank You God for setting me free. In Jesus' name I pray, Amen."

Is there anything specific that we can pray with you for? (Pray with them. Invite them to your church and get follow up info: name, address, & phone number.)

Our Goal?
Every Soul!

Daniel & Jessica King

KING MINISTRIES INTERNATIONAL

Soul Winning Festivals

Dominican Republic

Honduras

Panama

Mexico

Guatemala

Sudan

Brazil	Haiti
Pakistan	Indonesia
India	Haiti
South Africa	Columbia
Peru	Nicaragua

The MillionHeirs Club

When Daniel King was fifteen years old, he set a goal to lead 1,000,000 people to Jesus before his 30th birthday. Instead of trying to become a millionaire, he decided to lead a million "heirs" into the kingdom of God. *"If you belong to Christ then you are heirs"* (Galatians 3:29).

After celebrating the completion of this goal, Daniel & Jessica made it their mission to go for one million souls every year.

This **Quest for Souls** is accomplished through:
* Soul Winning Festivals
* Leadership Training
* Literature Distribution
* Humanitarian Relief

Would you help us lead people to Jesus by joining The MillionHeir's Club?

Visit www.kingministries.com to get involved!

6 Power-Packed Books

Healing Power

Do you need healing? This power-packed book contains 17 truths to activating your healing today!

(BK 02) $20.00

Fire Power

Inside these pages you will learn how to CATCH the fire of God, KEEP the fire of God, and SPREAD the fire of God!

(BK 01) $12.00

Soul Winning

Do you have a passion for the lost? This book shares over 150 truths about soul winning.

(BK 05) $10.00

The Secret of Obed-Edom

Unlock the secret to supernatural promotion and a more intimate walk with God. Unleash amazing blessing in your life!

(BK 06) $20.00

Power of the Seed

Discover the power of Seedtime & Harvest! Discover why your giving is the most important thing you will ever do!

(BK 04) $20.00

Welcome to the Kingdom

This is a perfect book for new believers. Learn how to be saved, healed, and delivered. (Available in bulk discounts)

(BK 03) $10.00

To Order Call: 1-877-431-4276 Write: PO Box 701113 Tulsa, OK 74170
Online: www.kingministries.com

Resources to Help You Grow

You can be Healed

When you need healing, listen to this CD. Discover the truths that will help you tap into God's healing power!

(CD 01) $15.00

The Blessing of Obed-Edom

This is the #1 message that the Body of Christ needs to hear. You will learn the explosive secrets to your supernatural promotion!

(DVD 01) $20.00

7 Reasons to be a Soulwinner

Daniel King's passion is to lead the lost to Christ. Learn how to ignite the same passion in your life. Plus: Practical tips for witnessing.

(CD 02) $15.00

Thinking Outside the BOX

God is not in the BOX. Learn why on this powerful CD that will change the way you think about God.

(CD 03) $15.00

Ignite

A must for those who want to ignite genuine passion for Jesus! Discover the keys to sparking your personal revival.

(CD 04) $15.00

Crowns

Do you wonder what your reward will be in heaven? This CD will explain how you can receive your eternal prize!

(CD 05) $15.00

To Order Call: 1-877-431-4276 Write: PO Box 701113 Tulsa, OK 74170
Online: www.kingministries.com

About the Author

Daniel King and his wife Jessica met in the middle of Africa while they were both on a mission trip. They are in high demand as speakers at churches and conferences all over North America. Their passion, energy, and enthusiasm are enjoyed by audiences everywhere they go.

They are international missionary evangelists who do massive soul winning festivals in countries around the world. Their passion for the lost has taken them to over fifty nations preaching the gospel to crowds that often exceed 50,000 people.

Daniel was called into the ministry when he was five years old and began to preach when he was six. His parents became missionaries to Mexico when he was ten. When he was fourteen he started a children's ministry that gave him the opportunity to minister in some of America's largest churches while still a teenager.

At the age of fifteen, Daniel read a book where the author encouraged young people to set a goal to earn $1,000,000. Daniel reinterpreted the message and determined to win 1,000,000 people to Christ every year. When he completed this goal, God told him to go for one million souls every year.

Daniel has authored ten books including his bestsellers Healing Power and Fire Power. His book Welcome to the Kingdom has been given away to tens of thousands of new believers.

KING MINISTRIES INTERNATIONAL

The vision of King Ministries is to bring 1,000,000 souls into the kingdom of God every year and to train believers to become leaders.

If you want Daniel King
to visit your church, write:
King Ministries International
PO Box 701113
Tulsa, OK 74170-1113

Call toll-free in North America:
1-877-431-4276

E-mail:
Daniel@kingministries.com

Visit us on the web at:
www.kingministries.com